STEVE JOBS

The Brilliant Mind Behind Apple

Life Portraits

STEVE JOBS
The Brilliant Mind Behind Apple

By Anthony Imbimbo

Gareth Stevens
Publishing

Please visit our web site at **www.garethstevens.com.**
For a free catalog describing Gareth Stevens Publishing's list of high-quality books,
call 1-800-542-2595 (USA) or 1-800-387-3178 (Canada).
Gareth Stevens Publishing's fax: 1-877-542-2596

Library of Congress Cataloging-in-Publication Data
Imbimbo, Anthony.
    Steve Jobs: the brilliant mind behind Apple / by Anthony Imbimbo.
        p. cm. — (Life portraits)
    Includes bibliographical references and index.
        ISBN-10: 1-4339-0060-2 / ISBN-13: 978-1-4339-0060-0 (lib. bdg.)
        1. Jobs, Steven, 1955- 2. Computer engineers—United States—Biography.
    3. Apple Computer, Inc. —History. I. Title.
    QA76.2.A2I53   2008
    621.39092—dc22
    [B]   2008041004

This edition first published in 2009 by
Gareth Stevens Publishing
A Weekly Reader® Company
1 Reader's Digest Rd.
Pleasantville, NY 10570-7000 USA

Executive Managing Editor: Lisa M. Herrington
Creative Director: Lisa Donovan
Cover Designer: Keith Plechaty
Interior Designers: Yin Ling Wong and Keith Plechaty
Publisher: Keith Garton

Produced by Spooky Cheetah Press
www.spookycheetah.com
Editor: Stephanie Fitzgerald
Designer: Kimberly Shake
Cartographer: XNR Productions, Inc.
Proofreader: Jessica Cohn
Indexer: Madge Walls, All Sky Indexing

Printed in the United States of America

1 2 3 4 5 6 7 8 9 12 11 10 09 08

TABLE OF CONTENTS

*Steve rocked the technology world when he presented
the iPhone at the 2007 Macworld Conference & Expo.*

CHAPTER ONE

Reinventing the Phone

A CROWD OF THOUSANDS FIXED THEIR EYES ON an empty stage. They were anxiously waiting for the star of the day to make an appearance. Finally, as music blared from loudspeakers, a middle-aged man dressed in blue jeans, sneakers, and a black turtleneck walked across the stage. The audience erupted into cheers and applause as he prepared to speak. If someone didn't know better, he or she might think the setting was a rock concert. In reality, though, the large crowd was gathered at a technology trade show. It was the 2007 Macworld Conference & Expo—a high-tech version of show and tell. The man on stage wasn't a rock star. He was a businessman in charge of a computer company that was ready to announce a major technological innovation.

Steve Jobs is the head of Apple Computer. He had come to San Francisco, California, to introduce Apple's latest high-tech gadget to the word. The world couldn't wait to see what it was. As he greeted the audience, Steve declared:

> *We're going to make some history together. ... This is a day I've been looking forward to for two and a half years. Every once in a while, a revolutionary product comes along that changes everything. One is very fortunate if you get the chance to work on just one of these in your career. Apple's been very fortunate. It's been able to introduce a few of these into the world. In 1984, we introduced the Macintosh. It didn't just change Apple. It changed the whole computer industry. In 2001, we introduced the first iPod. It didn't just change the way we all listen to music. It changed the entire music industry. Well, today, we're introducing three revolutionary products of this class.*

Steve introduced each new product one by one. The first was a revamped new widescreen iPod, the second an innovative new mobile phone, and the third an Internet communications device. As Steve mentioned each, cheers rose from the audience.

"So, three things: a widescreen iPod with touch controls, a revolutionary mobile phone, and a breakthrough Internet communications device," Steve repeated. Now, he paused after each word: "An iPod ... a phone ... and an Internet communicator." The image of each device spun into view on a giant video screen as it was mentioned. "An iPod ... a phone," Jobs hinted. "Are you getting it?" By this time, the excitement in the room had reached a fever pitch. Finally Steve gave the crowd what they

Welcome to Macworld

Held every year since 1985 in San Francisco, California, the Macworld Conference & Expo is the biggest event of the year for Mac users. The five-day trade show is where more than 400 companies, Apple included, introduce their new products.

Thousands of people attend the show to get a first look at hot new products. They also go to try out the products and meet the people who created them. The media attend Macworld, too. They share the news with the rest of the world.

The items on display at Macworld are all things a Mac owner might use—from computers and software to digital cameras and battery chargers.

In 1997, Steve Jobs began a tradition of giving the most important speech, or keynote address, at Macworld. These speeches, nicknamed "Stevenotes," usually reveal some big surprises, including product news or new plans for the company. Steve's address is usually the biggest attraction at Macworld.

were waiting for. "These are not three separate devices," he said. "This is one device, and we are calling it iPhone. Today, Apple is going to reinvent the phone."

Steve then demonstrated the amazing features of the iPhone. He turned it on, selected the iPod, and with a flick of his finger, scrolled through a long list of albums. Then he played a Beatles song. The iPhone's brilliant colors, large easy-to-see icons, wide screen, full keyboard for text messages, visible voice mail, access to the Internet, and Google Maps were among the many things that stood out as Steve showed off his new device. It truly was a revolutionary product.

People camped out at Apple stores across the country in order to be among the first to own an iPhone.

Phones Made Fun

One reason for the iPhone's existence is that Steve Jobs didn't like his old cell phone. Among the many things that annoyed him was the set of tiny buttons he had to press to send a text message or dial a number. Steve wanted to eliminate all the clunky features of regular mobile phones and make the iPhone more fun and effortless. With this in mind, Apple had the iPhone loaded with cool features such as the iPod and full Internet capabilities, as well as an extra-wide, touch-activated screen, a full keyboard for text messaging, and visible voice mail.

Almost immediately, news of Apple's iPhone began to spread. Television networks broadcast news of the iPhone, pointing out key features. One reporter gushed, "You can have your e-mail. You can have full Web browsing. It's got a very user-friendly interface." Those who didn't see or read these news reports were sure to see the TV ads that flooded the airwaves.

When iPhones made it to stores on June 29, 2007, they were a huge hit. People slept outside of Apple stores in the rain and summer heat just to be among the first to own one. More than a quarter million iPhones were sold the first weekend.

Apple had already given the world all kinds of innovations, including the Macintosh computer and the iPod—the sleek little device that stores and plays hundreds of songs. In 2007, Steve had worked his magic again. His company introduced a device that was more fun, functional, and better looking than anything else like it. Just as important, Steve used his incredible showmanship and genuine passion for technology to make the iPhone one of the most popular and successful new products of the year.

AN UNLIKELY JOURNEY

It's amazing to think that 31 years earlier, Steve was a college dropout living with his parents and selling computers out of his garage. Even more amazing—he had become a millionaire at age 24. As a kid, Steve was bored with school, but he was incredibly smart and hardworking, and he had a fascination for and a deep understanding of computer electronics. His imagination allowed him to see the full value of these machines before others could. Back then, most computers were monstrous machines available primarily to big businesses, colleges, and government agencies. Steve imagined how awesome it would be if everyone could have their very own personal computer. So he and his friend Steve "Woz" Wozniak developed one. They called their personal computer the Apple, and it changed everything. The Apple put the power of computing into the hands of ordinary people everywhere, opening up a world of discovery and innovation that continues to this day.

Steve never stopped thinking about ways to improve the computer, or of new ways to harness the power of computing. This passion led him to develop many features that computer users now take for granted, such as the mouse, different kinds of fonts, and a computer screen that can display graphics. Not

Steve Jobs got his start selling computers that his friends assembled in his family's garage in 1976.

all of Steve's ideas were successful. In fact, some were flops. Nevertheless, he always trusted that his curiosity would lead him in the right direction, and for the most part, it has. His influence now extends from computers to music to telephones and even to the movies.

Steve's success has made him very famous—and very wealthy. It was neither fame nor fortune that drove him to work so hard, however. Curiosity, imagination, and the joy of discovery have motivated Steve throughout his life. His journey of discovery began when he was very young and continues even now. ❖

When Steve was a kid, he spent many hours working alongside his dad in the family's garage. Steve fiddled with electronics while his dad worked on cars.

CHAPTER TWO

EARLY PROMISE

O N FEBRUARY 24, 1955, A YOUNG COLLEGE student in San Francisco gave birth to a son. Unmarried and not yet ready for parenthood, she decided it would be best if she gave her child up for adoption. The young woman wanted a good future for the boy. To her, that meant a college education. So she insisted that the child be adopted by college graduates. When the adoption agency found a college-educated lawyer and his wife who wanted to raise a son, it seemed like a perfect match.

Then, at the last minute, the couple had a change of heart. They wanted a girl instead. The adoption agency worked very quickly to find another set of parents. Paul and Clara Jobs were next on the waiting list. Once again, however, there was a problem. Neither Paul nor Clara were college graduates. In fact, Paul Jobs never even graduated from high school. When the birth mother found out, she refused to let the couple adopt her son. She eventually agreed to give up the child on one condition. Paul and Clara had to promise to send the boy to college. The Jobses agreed. They named their new son Steven Paul Jobs.

A GROWING FAMILY

When Steve was 2 years old, the Jobses adopted a little girl. Steve's sister was named Patty. The family lived in south San Francisco, an industrial part of the city with factories and small, modest homes. Paul, who was a machinist, had a special passion for cars. He sold used cars, worked for a company that made car loans, and in his spare time, liked to tinker with cars. He would buy old, broken-down vehicles, fix them up, and sell them for a profit. Steve remembered:

> He had a workbench out in his garage where, when I was about five or six, he sectioned off a little piece of it and said 'Steve, this is your workbench now.' And he gave me some of his smaller tools and showed me how to use a hammer and saw, and how to build things. One of the things he touched upon was electronics. He did not have a deep understanding of electronics himself but he'd encountered electronics a lot in automobiles and other things he would fix. He showed me the rudiments of electronics and I got very interested in that.

Clara Jobs spent most of her time raising her children. Steve, for one, certainly kept her busy. The little boy liked to wake up before dawn. To keep him quiet until everyone else was ready to get up, Steve's parents bought him a rocking horse, a record player, and Little Richard records. Steve, who had an incredibly curious nature, also had a knack for getting into things. He once burned his hand by sticking a bobby pin into an electrical outlet. It was his first—very painful—introduction to electronics.

As he grew a little older, Steve demonstrated that he was a quick learner. "My mother taught me how to read before I got to school," Steve said, "so when I got there, I really wanted to do just two things. I wanted to read books because I loved reading books and I wanted to go outside and chase butterflies."

THE MISCHIEF-MAKER

By third grade, Steve's family had moved to Mountain View, California, just south of San Francisco. Steve took music lessons and competed on the Mountain View Country Club swim team. He was bored at school, though, and that boredom turned into mischief. Steve and his friend Rick Farentino played a lot of pranks. One time they set off explosives in the teacher's desk. "We got kicked out of school a lot," Steve later admitted.

Steve was also strong-willed and refused to do schoolwork that he considered a waste of time. If it weren't for his fourth grade teacher, Steve may have had an entirely different future. The teacher, Imogene "Teddy" Hill, recognized how bright Steve was and found ways to motivate him to do his work. "I really want you to finish this workbook," she would tell him. "I'll give you five bucks if you fin-

> **"We got kicked out of school a lot."**
>
> – STEVE JOBS

Steve grew up near Silicon Valley—the perfect setting for someone with a deep interest in computers and electronics and the drive to revolutionize the industry.

ish it." The little bribes, along with Teddy's encouragement and her belief in his ability, changed Steve's study habits. He started performing brilliantly. Steve did so well in fourth grade that his teachers recommended he skip fifth grade. "I'm 100% sure that if it hadn't been for Mrs. Hill in fourth grade and a few others, I absolutely would have ended up in jail," Steve said years later.

FRIENDS AND NEIGHBORS

Steve was getting an education outside of the classroom, too. Santa Clara County was home to Stanford University and many high-technology firms. Also known as Silicon Valley, because it was where the silicon chip was developed, the area attracted many of the country's brightest engineers. One of those engineers, Larry Lange, was a neighbor of the Jobs family. Mr. Lange, a Hewlett-Packard employee, liked to tinker with electronic devices in his garage. He kept his garage door open, almost as

Silicon Valley

Technology companies began popping up in Santa Clara Valley as early as 1909, many of which served the U.S. Navy and its local air base, Moffett Field. In the 1940s, Stanford University lured more tech firms to the valley by renting land to them. One of the first companies to set up shop was Hewlett-Packard. The concentration of brilliant scientists and engineers in the area gave rise to new inventions and businesses looking to profit from them. Companies like Fairchild Semiconductor and Intel led the way in developing silicon computer chips, and by the 1970s, the area came to be known as Silicon Valley. It has been attracting computer and software companies, from Apple to Yahoo! to Google, ever since.

Hewlett-Packard

The Hewlett-Packard company was founded in 1939 by Bill Hewlett and Dave Packard. The two Stanford University graduates started their business from a Palo Alto garage. Their garage had a work area, a bedroom for Dave and his

wife, and a sleeping shed for Bill. They specialized in making devices that tested and measured electronic equipment. Their first big success was an oscillator used for testing audio equipment.

The garage where Bill Hewlett and Dave Packard started their business is now a historic landmark.

As Hewlett-Packard grew into one of the largest electronics companies in the country, it established a reputation for developing innovative technology and fostering creativity among its workers. Hewlett and Packard encouraged their employees to work collaboratively and to pursue inventions of their own. They offered flexible working hours and acted as mentors to young inventors. That creative spirit spread throughout the valley. So did the feeling that anyone with a bright idea and a garage could start a successful business, just as Bill and Dave had.

an invitation to any curious person who walked by. Steve passed by often, and he was curious. He would watch Mr. Lange piece together electronic parts, run a current through them, and then, *poof,* produce light or sound! The boy felt like he was watching a magician at work. Steve was thrilled when Mr. Lange gave him a carbon microphone that could amplify sound without being plugged into an amplifier.

Electronic gadgets absolutely amazed Steve. He spent count-less hours in Mr. Lange's garage building them and learning about them. Mr. Lange was impressed by the way Steve could focus on a project for a long period of time. The boy was determined to figure out how to put a device together and understand how it worked. Recognizing Steve's interest in electronics, Mr. Lange recommended that he become a member of Hewlett-Packard's Explorers Club. The kids' group met Tuesday evenings in the company cafeteria, where they would get an up-close look at the company's latest inventions. For a young techy like Steve, this was like watching a major league baseball game from inside the

> **"You looked at a television set, you would think that 'I haven't built one of those, but I could.'"**
>
> – STEVE JOBS

dugout. You couldn't get much closer to the action than this. Between the Explorers Club and the Lange garage, Steve was getting an education in electronics that was far superior to what he would find in a science class. "These things were not mysteries anymore," he said. "I mean, you looked at a television set, you would think that 'I haven't built one of those, but I could.'"

MORE TROUBLE AT SCHOOL

When Steve advanced to the sixth grade, he enrolled at Crittenden Middle School. Students at Crittenden were rough and rowdy. Gangs would sometimes get into fights, and the police were often called in to break them up. Paul and Clara Jobs feared that their son was getting pulled into situations that were over his head. Because he skipped fifth grade, Steve was a year younger than his classmates. He didn't seem to fit in, and he had trouble making friends. Not surprisingly, Steve came to hate his new school. After finishing sixth grade, he refused to go back to Crittenden. Steve's parents didn't want to force him, nor did they think Crittenden would be a good school for Patty. They decided it would be best if they moved to a new school district. So they picked up and headed a few miles west to nearby Los Altos, California.

As he settled in Los Altos, Steve became friends with classmate Bill Fernandez. The two boys shared an interest in electronics, and Bill's garage served as a terrific workshop. After school they would stop at Bill's house, hang out in the garage, and tinker with electronic gadgets. Bill had another friend who lived down the street: Steve Wozniak. "Woz" knew even more about electronics than Steve or Bill did. Woz was five years older than Bill and Steve. He was a senior in high school, and he had already won a number of electronics fairs. Whenever Bill needed help designing one of his electronic devices, he would turn to his older friend for assistance.

Bill raved about Woz's talents and told Steve that he would introduce him to Woz. Bill knew the two Steves would get along great, but he never imagined that his friends would one day make

The Two Steves

Steve Jobs and Steve Wozniak got along from the moment they met. "Steve and I just sat ... for the longest time just sharing stories," Woz recalled. "We talked electronics, we talked about music we liked, and we traded stories about pranks we pulled." Woz often had a difficult

Steve and Woz (shown here in 1977) realized they made a great team soon after they met.

time explaining the complex gadgets he was working on, confusing listeners with electronics terms and concepts, but Steve understood Woz perfectly. "Steve got it right away, and I liked him," Woz recalled. Woz knew more about electrical engineering, while Steve was more articulate and outgoing; so they made a good team.

computer history together as the founders of Apple Computer. When Steve and Woz first met, they were both teenagers. Just a decade later, they would lead a high-tech revolution. ❖

The first time Steve saw a desktop computer he knew it was something special. Ten years later, he and Woz would revolutionize the computing world with the Apple computer.

CHAPTER THREE

WIREHEADS

A FTER MOVING TO LOS ALTOS, STEVE CONTINUED to make the 15-minute trip to Hewlett-Packard's office for Explorers Club meetings. He loved to see what cool devices the engineers would share with the group. Sometimes they would show how a product like a calculator worked. Other times they would present prototypes of holograms or other high-tech ideas that were in development. When he was 12 years old, Steve saw one product that made a lasting impression. "I saw my first desktop computer at Hewlett-Packard," he recalled. "It was the first desktop in the world. I fell in love with it."

Explorers Club members shared ideas and inspired each other to come up with clever gadgets of their own. As he worked on these projects, Steve began to uncover more of the secrets of electrical engineering. He was also becoming more aware of his own unique talents.

Early Computers

Computers of the 1960s were monstrous, each the size of a refrigerator. Used by businesses and government agencies, these mainframe computers ran programs that were written on a series of hole-punched cards coded with data. One of the most popular computer models of the time was IBM's S/360. These models came with separate disk drives that were the size of washing machines! At 14 inches (35.6 centimeters) in diameter, the disks themselves were bigger than dinner plates. They came in stacks that weighed as much as a bowling ball, or about 10 pounds (4.5 kilograms). One disk could hold a little more than 7 megabytes. This was a lot at the time, but it would barely store six digital photos today.

The IBM 360 was a huge computer.

A SUMMER JOB

Making a computer or any kind of electronic device requires the right set of parts. For a teen with no money, acquiring those parts wasn't easy, but Steve was developing a talent for it. One time, Steve was building a frequency counter. He realized he was missing key components and knew that Hewlett-Packard was sure to have them. It couldn't hurt, he thought, to ask the company for them. Steve scanned the phone book and found the number for Bill Hewlett. Hewlett was one of the owners of the company, but Steve didn't let that stop him. He dialed up Mr. Hewlett and asked him for the parts. By the end of the conversation, Mr. Hewlett agreed to give Steve the parts for free—and offered the 13-year-old a job! Steve remembers:

> *[Bill Hewlett] didn't know me at all, but he ended up giving me some parts, and he got me a job that summer working at Hewlett-Packard on the line, assembling frequency counters. Assembling may be too strong [a word]. I was putting in screws.*

Steve's ability to talk intelligently and passionately about electronics opened doors for him. His confidence made others believe in him. Throughout Steve's life, these traits would energize the people he worked with and break down barriers. Thanks to his can-do spirit and willingness to work hard, Steve landed a job at one of the leading tech firms in the nation the summer before he started high school. Even though it was tedious assembly line work, Steve didn't mind. "I was in heaven," he recalled.

NEW DIRECTIONS

When Steve enrolled at Homestead High School that fall, he began a journey that would take him in new directions. He started out on familiar footing. As a freshman, he enrolled in an advanced electronics class with his friend Bill Fernandez. Prior to high school, Steve's understanding of electronics came from watching people like Larry Lange and the engineers at the Explorers Club piece together electronic devices. By observing and by making gadgets of his own, Steve learned *how* electronic devices work. In high school, his teacher began to help him understand *why* these devices worked. He was learning the scientific principles of electrical engineering.

Steve also joined the school's electronics club. Members of the club were called "wireheads." At Homestead High, wireheads were pretty cool. They made stuff, entered it in science fairs, and very often won. Wireheads also pulled off some of the most memorable school pranks, which made the club even more appealing to a prankster like Steve.

Bill became a wirehead, too. He spent his spare time after his sophomore year helping his buddy Woz build a computer

Bill Fernandez (left) was a friend of both Steve and Woz long before the three wireheads started working together in the 1970s.

from scratch. Woz had been studying computer programming at De Anza College, in Cupertino, and working for a local computer company. He had also been researching computer design, poring over computer manuals, and sketching out designs for circuit boards, the network of circuits that forms the brains of the machine. When Woz's employer gave him some parts to use, he and Bill began to make a computer.

> "[Woz] was the first person I met who knew more [about] electronics than I did."
>
> – STEVE JOBS

Woz would figure out what parts were needed and where they should go, and Bill would help assemble the parts. The computer couldn't do much more than process simple commands, but it was a working computer, and it made a huge impression on Steve. "I could tell he was impressed," Woz said. "I mean, we'd actually built a computer from scratch and proved it was possible—or going to be possible—for people to have computers in a really small space." Steve realized how much thought and hard work went into the design of Woz's machine. He also recognized that Woz had a special talent for electrical engineering. "He was the first person I met who knew more [about] electronics than I did," Steve recalled.

That was high praise coming from Steve, who knew quite a bit about electronics himself. After his second year in high school, Steve started a weekend job at an electronic parts store called Haltek. This was where wireheads and other electronics buffs bought supplies for their projects. The store carried a huge assortment of parts. Over time, Steve came to learn what all the

The Cream Soda Computer

Woz called his computer the "Flair pen" or "cream soda" computer. That's because he used a Flair pen to sketch out the design, and he and Bill Fernandez drank a lot of cream soda while they were building it. Woz's computer was very basic. It consisted of a hand-sized circuit board with eight computer chips and some plug-in connectors. It had a front panel of eight lights, eight switches, and an enter button. Programs were written onto hole-punched cards and read by the computer. The computer could carry out only simple commands, like beep three times. But Woz proved to himself that he could design a computer for personal use. He found a kindred spirit in Steve Jobs, who was eager to discover where this technology might lead.

parts were used for, how much they cost, and how to recognize good quality. With this knowledge, he could find secondhand parts and bargain with the seller for a low price. Then he would fix the part and resell it for a profit. These were negotiating skills he learned while watching his dad buy parts for the cars he rebuilt. By working at Haltek and selling parts in his spare time, Steve managed to save enough money to buy a used car when he was 15 years old. More importantly, his encyclopedic knowledge of electronic components and his negotiating skills would help him in many future business dealings.

A NEW FRIEND

Steve was not interested just in electronics. He also played the trumpet in the marching band. As he advanced through high school, Steve developed a taste for all kinds of music, from the Beatles to Beethoven. He also liked to read and came to appreciate literary classics such as the works of William Shakespeare and poet Dylan Thomas. Like many teenagers of the time, Steve also became aware of social issues like poverty and the environment. His appearance—torn jeans and shoulder-length hair—began to reflect the rebellious spirit of the 1960s and '70s, as well as his youthful defiance and individualism. It was during this time that Steve met Chris-Ann Brennan. Chris-Ann liked Steve's mischievousness. They shared many of the same friends and found they had much in common. They shared an interest in the arts and enjoyed taking in the natural beauty and solitude

Steve had many hobbies in addition to electronics. He also loved music and played trumpet in his high school marching band.

of the nearby beaches and mountain ranges. Their relationship would continue, off and on, even after high school.

By his senior year, Steve also began spending more time with Woz. Woz was enrolled at the University of California at Berkeley, about 30 minutes away in San Francisco. Steve would drive to visit him there, or Woz would come down to the valley—often to help with one of Steve's latest pranks. One day, Woz read a magazine article about a group of people, called "phone phreaks," who figured out how to make long distance telephone calls for free. These hackers discovered that the tone of high E, or 2,600 hertz, could free up a telephone line. All they

At the 2007 Macworld, Steve stood in front of a piece of history. The photo shows Steve and Woz at work on the very first Apple computer.

had to do was dial a toll-free prefix, like 800, and then emit the sound and the line would open. Once the line was available, they could duplicate the tones for the actual phone number and the call would go through.

One hacker had created a device in a blue box that could transmit the proper signals. When Woz and Steve learned how it worked, they decided to make a "blue box" of their own. Woz designed a digital model that could produce the exact tones needed to make a long distance call, and Steve suggested that they sell them. They used $40 worth of parts and sold the gadgets for between $150 (for college students) and $300 (everyone else). They peddled their blue boxes from dorm to dorm at nearby colleges and by word of mouth all around the area. They made a nifty profit. The devices were illegal, of course. Steve and Woz realized that the more popular their blue boxes became the more likely it was they would get caught. So they stopped. It was Steve and Woz's first business together. It wouldn't be their last.

Meanwhile, Steve's parents never lost sight of their promise to send him to college. His mom worked as an accountant, and his dad worked as a machinist at a company that made lasers. Paul Jobs also continued to work on cars. He bought junkers for $50, fixed them up, and then sold them for a profit. Whatever money Paul earned, he saved. "That," Steve recalls, "was my college fund." ❖

Although his parents hoped Steve would attend a less expensive school, he was determined to attend Reed College in Portland, Oregon.

CHAPTER FOUR

FINDING HIS WAY

WHEN IT CAME TIME TO CHOOSE A COLLEGE, Steve set his sights on Reed College, a small liberal arts school in Portland, Oregon. One of the top small schools in the country, Reed was also one of the most expensive. Any of California's outstanding state schools would have been more affordable for a state resident like Steve. The strong-willed teenager wanted to be far from home and on his own, however. In fact, he insisted on it. Steve told his parents that if he couldn't go to Reed, he wouldn't go to any college. So, despite the financial burden, Paul and Clara paid Steve's tuition bill and drove him to Portland.

Unfortunately, once Steve arrived on campus, he showed more interest in learning "what life was all about," as he put it, than he did in the subjects he was required to take. He attended classes when he felt like it and made a weak attempt at mastering the demanding course work. His poor grades reflected his lack of effort. Steve's parents insisted that he had to improve his grades to justify the expense of college. Instead, after six months of school, Steve decided to drop out. He later recalled:

> *I couldn't see the value in it. I had no idea what I wanted to do with my life and no idea of how college was going to help me figure it out. And here I was spending all of the money my parents had saved their entire life. So I decided to drop out and trust that it would all work out okay.*

A FREE EDUCATION

Steve didn't drop out completely, however. The college allowed him to audit classes for free. Steve could attend a class and do all the assignments, but he would not receive credit toward a degree. This arrangement freed Steve from having to take the school's required set of courses. He could choose whatever classes interested him. One of the subjects that Steve studied was calligraphy, the art of decorative handwriting. He remembered:

> *Reed College at that time offered perhaps the best calligraphy instruction in the country. Throughout the campus, every poster, every label on every drawer, was beautifully hand calligraphed. Because I had dropped out and didn't have to take the normal classes, I decided to take a calligraphy class to learn how to do this. I learned about serif and sans serif typefaces,*

about varying the amount of space between different letter combinations, about what makes great typography great.

Many years later, Steve's knowledge of calligraphy would lead him to make computers that used different kinds of fonts, or letter styles. At the time, however, no such thoughts entered his mind. Steve just wanted to learn about the art for its own sake. "It was beautiful, historical, artistically subtle in a way that science can't capture," he said, "and I found it fascinating."

Steve continued taking classes at Reed for the rest of the school year. He couldn't see wasting his parents' money while

Calligraphy

Calligraphy is the art of writing beautifully. Its various forms have been practiced all through the ages and by people all over the world, from the ancient Chinese to monks of the Middle Ages to the ancient Maya. Calligraphy was one of the most popular classes at Reed College. In addition to Steve Jobs, Reed calligraphy students included Chuck Bigelow and Kris Holmes, who created the Lucida typeface and many others. Every Macintosh computer includes fonts created by Bigelow and Holmes. "If I had never dropped in on that single course in college," Steve has said, "the Mac would have never had multiple typefaces or proportionally spaced fonts."

deciding what to do with his life, so Steve tried to make it on his own. He couldn't afford a dorm room, so he would sleep on the floor of a friend's room. He had very little money for food, so he would collect bottles and return them for the five-cent refund. On Sundays, he would walk seven miles to a Hare Krishna temple for a free meal—his one balanced meal of the week. None of these hardships seemed to bother Steve. "I loved it," he said.

ON HIS OWN

Steve stayed on campus during the summer when his friends went home. He earned money by repairing lab equipment for the psychology department. This allowed him to rent a small apartment for $25 a month. It was important to Steve that he live on his own—and that he live the way he wanted to live. Steve rarely wore shoes or washed his clothes; his jeans had holes in them; and his hair was long. He cared little for material things. Instead, Steve wondered about the big questions of life. He became more curious about his biological parents and even attempted to find them. He also wondered about his purpose in life and explored Eastern philosophies and religions for answers.

When classes started again, Steve audited new courses. On weekends, he and his friends attended spiritual retreats at the All-One Farm in Oregon. Visitors to the farm got the chance to experience self-reliance by living a simpler life, closer to nature. They grew their own food and worked to make the farm's apple orchards and wheat fields prosper. For his part, Steve tended a neglected apple orchard until it was bearing healthy quantities of fruit again. Among the many visitors to the farm was Steve's

Steve found great satisfaction in restoring a neglected apple orchard at the All-One Farm. He would later recall the experience when choosing a name for his company.

high school girlfriend, Chris-Ann Brennan. They were no longer dating but remained friends. Their brief reunion at the farm happened by chance, but they would see each other again.

A NEW JOB

By the middle of what would have been Steve's sophomore year, he had an urge to travel. Lacking the money for a trip, he returned to his parents' home in the spring of 1974 and started looking for a job. As he searched the want ads one day, Steve saw one that read, "Have fun and make money." A company called Atari was hiring technicians to help them develop video games.

Atari had recently introduced a video game called *Pong*, which had become a big hit. The company planned to reinvest its huge profits by making more games. Atari needed electronics technicians and engineers to develop these games, and Steve applied for the job—in his typical unique fashion. When he showed up at Atari, the rumpled-looking hippie told the personnel director that he wouldn't leave the building until he was hired. That message was passed along to Atari's chief engineer, Al Alcorn. Alcorn took time to speak to Steve and, afterward, offered him the position. "I don't know why I hired him," Alcorn said, "except that he was determined to have the job, and there was some spark, some inner energy, an attitude that he was going to get it done."

> **"I don't know why I hired [Steve], except there was some spark, some inner energy, an attitude that he was going to get it done."**
>
> **– AL ALCORN, ATARI'S CHIEF ENGINEER**

Steve's untidy look, along with the insulting way he spoke to his coworkers, made other Atari employees dislike him. They complained to management about Steve's rudeness. To minimize the complaints, Alcorn had Steve work the night shift, a time when almost no one else was in the office.

While working at Atari, Steve began making plans for a trip to India. He wanted to immerse himself in the Hindu way of life as part of his continuing quest for spiritual fulfillment. He had two problems, though: He couldn't afford the trip, and he had a job. Steve was never easily discouraged, though. He just asked his boss for the money—and for the time off from work!

Atari Video Games

Atari was America's first successful video game company. In 1972, it introduced *Pong*, a video game that simulated table tennis (or Ping Pong). It became an instant sensation. The game was popular in arcades, where people lined up to play. *Pong's* popularity led Atari to develop a home version. For Christmas 1975, the *Pong* home console, sold exclusively by Sears, was one of the hits of the season, selling out at stores across the nation.

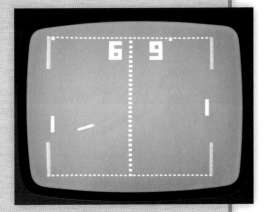

Atari went on to also develop personal computers, but it was video games that made the company such a big success. Its most popular games included *Breakout, Football, Asteroids,* and

Compared to today's video games, Pong was hardly high-tech. It was the first game of is kind, though, and a huge sensation.

Centipede. The company's founders, Nolan Bushnell and Ted Dabney, sold Atari to Warner Communications in 1976 for roughly $28 million. By the mid 1980s, however, the popularity of Atari games began to wane. Over time, other video game makers such as Nintendo and Sony began to take the lead in innovation.

At first Alcorn laughed at him. Then he thought about it. Atari's German distributor was having trouble wiring the Atari games that were sold in that country. If Steve stopped in Germany to fix the wiring problem, Atari would pay for the trip. Steve agreed.

A JOURNEY OF DISCOVERY

In the summer of 1974, Steve and his college friend Dan Kottke set out on a month-long journey to meet spiritual leaders in India. What they found was a land where poverty and hardship were more severe than anything they'd ever seen before. Steve abandoned his material possessions and had his head shaved. He also attended religious festivals and met Hindu gurus, or teachers. These experiences gave Steve insight into a world he had never known before. Unfortunately, they failed to provide the great spiritual awakening he hoped to find. The Hindu teacher Steve and Dan wanted to learn more about, Neem Karoli Baba, had died months earlier, and people were trying to profit from his popularity. Steve came to an important realization. Great ideas without action suddenly seemed empty. He later explained:

> We weren't going to find a place where we could go for a month to be enlightened. It was one of the first times that I started to realize that maybe Thomas Edison did a lot more to improve the world than Karl Marx and [guru] Neem Karoli Baba put together.

Steve returned to California a more mature young man. He remained close with his friends from Reed College and continued to visit the All-One Farm. He would also continue his

A Life of Love

Neem Karoli Baba was a Hindu teacher who became popular in the United States after some of his American followers returned from India and spread the word about him. Dr. Richard Alpert, who changed his name to Ram Dass, was one such follower. Dass's book, *Miracles of Love*, described the teachings of Neem Karoli Baba, which emphasized living a life of love and truth. Another follower of Neem Karoli Baba, Dr.

Larry Brilliant later became the director of Google.org, the branch of Google that donates money to charitable causes.

Larry Brilliant, partnered with Ram Dass to start the Seva Foundation, an organization devoted to ending poverty. Seva was partly funded by a donation from Steve Jobs, who was a friend of Brilliant's.

search for his biological parents and greater spiritual well-being. After spending roughly two years away from home taking college courses, tending an apple orchard, and traveling to India, Steve's desire to "find the meaning of life" gave way to a much stronger need to do something meaningful with his life. ❖

Steve might not have looked the part, but by the late 1970s, he was on his way to becoming a giant of the computer industry.

CHAPTER FIVE

BREAKING OUT ON HIS OWN

S TEVE RETURNED TO ATARI IN THE FALL OF 1974. He was glad to be back, but his unusual habits continued to be an issue. Steve had a tendency to insult coworkers by telling them how poorly they did their jobs. "He was causing so much trouble ... that I had to step in and do something," recalls Atari owner Nolan Bushnell. The company put up with Steve's behavior because he was a good technician. In fact, it wasn't long before he was promoted to engineer. Steve was made a special consultant to Bushnell—he worked on projects for the owner rather than regular tasks. He also worked nights when fewer people were in the office.

Steve didn't mind the night shift. His friend Woz, who worked nearby at Hewlett-Packard, often visited him on the job. Woz would play video games and give Steve a hand with any electronics problem that came up. Working nights also gave Steve free time during the day to do other things that interested him. At the time, Steve was attending meditation sessions at the Los Altos Zen Center. Zen is a form of Buddhism that emphasizes meditation to free the mind of unproductive thoughts and to improve self-understanding. At the Zen Center, Steve met Kobin Chino, a Buddhist monk who became a lifelong mentor to him. These sessions helped Steve develop skills to focus his talents and energy in a more positive way. Steve also ran into his old girlfriend, Chris-Ann Brennan, at the Zen Center. They hadn't seen each other in months, but soon they started dating again. Steve also continued to make trips to the All-One Farm to visit friends and help with farm work.

THE HOMEBREW COMPUTER CLUB

Then, in early 1975, when Steve was just turning 20 years old, an issue of *Popular Electronics* magazine sent a buzz through the wirehead community. The magazine featured a cover story about a do-it-yourself computer called the Altair. It was a package of components and instructions that allowed techies to build their own computer, and it cost about $400. People in the electronics field, accustomed to using large mainframe computers at work, were thrilled at the thought of constructing their own smaller machines. Roughly 4,000 kits were sold in the month after the article appeared. Shortly after that, an organization called the Homebrew Computer Club was formed. The club made it possible for hobbyists around the Silicon Valley to share their kits, as well as their talents for building the machines and making them work better.

The success of Altair sparked others to develop kits. They also developed components that made the computers more useful. Bill Gates and Paul Allen, the future founders of Microsoft, developed a programming language called Altair BASIC. This program allowed Altair users to write coded instructions to perform different functions on their computers. Another company sold integrated circuits that could be added to the machines to

Popular Electronics
magazine introduced the wirehead world to the first minicomputer kit.

boost the memory of the computers. As the functionality of the computers grew, Steve began to think of different ways to use the machines. He thought of how he might use a computer to develop computer games like the ones he was making at Atari.

Meanwhile, Woz's skills as a computer designer were becoming obvious to the other members of the Homebrew Computer Club. After one meeting, a local businessman asked Woz to help him start a company. Woz's job would be to make terminals that people could use to link to a large mainframe computer through a phone line. Woz said yes, but he insisted that Steve work on the project, too. It was a first step toward a personal computer, and Steve was glad to be part of the project.

BASIC: Language of Computers

All computer programs run on a set of coded instructions. The BASIC programming language made it easier to write those programs. In 1964, a pair of Dartmouth University professors, John Kemeny and Thomas Kurtz, created BASIC so that their students could use a computer without each one having to write a separate system of coded instructions. BASIC came with basic codes and commands that students could use to build more complex programs.

BASIC was also adaptable to different kinds of computers. In 1975, after learning about the Altair computer kit, Bill Gates and Paul Allen developed a version of BASIC specifically for that machine. Their version, Altair BASIC, became widely popular among computer hobbyists. Steve Wozniak created a version of BASIC for the Apple, called Apple BASIC. Over time, more than 200 different versions, or dialects, of BASIC were created, which is more than were created for any other programming language.

Woz wanted to keep his job at Hewlett-Packard and design the terminal in his spare time. Steve worked nights, so he could devote his days to buying parts, overseeing manufacturing, and managing the business. By the end of the project, the two friends had gained valuable experience making this new product and working together. They realized that they made a good team.

BUSINESS PARTNERS

In the fall of 1975, Steve took time off from work to help out with the apple harvest at the All-One Farm. When he returned, he checked in on Woz, who was designing a computer of his own. Woz's computer was nothing like the Altair. His machine was connected to a TV monitor and a keyboard. It would allow users to type in the BASIC programming language and write programs. Steve instantly recognized the value of the machine. It was a tool every computer hobbyist could use to develop new ways to process data, crunch numbers, and create all kinds of new programs.

Steve noticed how popular Woz's machine was among hobbyists. At Homebrew meetings, Woz was giving away his computer designs, or schematics, for free, and many hobbyists took them home. Then Steve noticed something else amazing. "The people at Homebrew," Steve told Woz, "are taking the schematics, but they don't have the time or the ability to build the computer."

Steve pointed out to Woz that people would buy this technology and suggested that the two of them start a business together. The idea was to sell just the printed circuit boards—the backbone of Woz's machine—for $50 each. Each board would have all the electrical wiring built right into it, and it would map out where all the computer chips should go. People could just solder the chips in the right spots, like using a paint-by-numbers kit. This way, the hobbyists at Homebrew could make a computer in days instead of weeks. Since the boards would only cost $25 each, Woz and Steve would make $25 with each sale. Woz could work at Hewlett-Packard during the day and design the circuit

Woz's Computer

When Woz saw the Altair, it reminded him of the computer he had built years earlier. It had no keyboard or monitor, just a display panel with lights. The one new thing it had was a microprocessor—a central processing unit (CPU) on

a single chip. Woz had built his CPU using a network of integrated circuits. Now the same kind of circuitry was available on a single chip. This technology, which had just been developed, made small personal computers possible.

Steve Wozniak in 1985

Woz knew all he had to do was write a program telling the CPU how to interpret keystrokes and display them on a TV screen. For this program, he used read-only memory (ROM) chips. These chips retain data, even when the computer is turned off, and allow the computer to start up the instant it's turned on. Woz got the idea from calculators, which use the same kind of memory chips. He also used random-access memory (RAM) chips, which temporarily store the information people type on their computers and can be accessed at any time. These features had never been combined like this until Woz's computer.

boards during the evenings. Steve would oversee manufacturing and sales during the day.

The two friends sat in Steve's car deciding their future. Woz recalled: "I can remember [Steve's] saying this like it was yesterday: 'Well, even if we lose our money, we'll have a company. For once in our lives, we'll have a company.'"

Woz was convinced. They would be equal partners and share 90 percent of the business. The other 10 percent went to a third partner, an artist named Ron Wayne who worked with Steve at Atari. Ron would write the instruction manual, design the logo, write ads, and do testing. The group needed a name, and Steve came up with Apple Computer. The apple was his favorite fruit, and his favorite rock band, the Beatles, recorded music for Apple Records. At the All-One Farm, Steve worked hard to make apples grow. Now he had to see if he and his friends could make Apple Computer grow, too.

OPEN FOR BUSINESS

In April 1976, Steve, Woz, and Ron signed the legal papers that established their new business. After the circuit board was created, Steve introduced the product, called the Apple I, at a meeting of the Homebrew Computer Club. To his disappointment, no one was interested—at least not in buying the empty circuit boards. There was one man, Paul Terrell, who had seen Woz's machine and approached Steve with a different kind of offer. Terrell owned a computer

> "Well, even if we lose our money, we'll have a company. For once in our lives, we'll have a company."
>
> – STEVE JOBS TO WOZ

store called the Byte Shop. He wanted to sell Woz's machine in his store. Terrell told Steve that he would buy 50 computers—fully assembled—for $500 each. That was a $25,000 order. Apple Computer was in business! Steve immediately phoned Woz to tell him the news. "Nothing in subsequent years was so great and so unexpected," Woz later recalled.

The two friends began scrambling to get the machines built. They bought the parts on credit. They hired friends Bill Fernandez and Dan Kottke and Steve's sister, Patty, to load components onto the circuit boards. Working out of Steve's house, they assembled the guts of each machine—the integrated circuits, the microprocessor, and the memory array. Ron created the manual and the logo, which featured a picture of inventor Sir Isaac Newton sitting under an apple tree.

To Steve and Woz, a "fully assembled computer" meant a printed circuit board with the chips, integrated circuits, and memory attached. It didn't include a keyboard, monitor, or even a case. When they had a dozen fully assembled circuit boards ready, Steve delivered them to the Byte Shop. Terrell was

The Apple I was little more than a circuit board. Steve designed a wooden case, but it had to be ordered separately.

expecting whole computers in a case with a keyboard and monitor. It was a big misunderstanding. To resolve the issue, Steve agreed to help Terrell order the other parts for the computers. Steve also agreed to design a case. Finally, Terrell asked that Steve create an interface card—a device that would allow users to install the BASIC programming language on a tape rather than having to type it in each time the computer was turned on. Steve agreed, and Terrell paid $500 each for the fully assembled circuit boards that day. Steve left the Byte Shop with $6,000. It was Apple Computer's first sale.

Steve and Woz and the rest of the crew worked on making the changes that Terrell wanted. Steve designed a wooden case for the machine, and Woz created the interface card. Keyboards and monitors were sold separately. Even in this rudimentary form, by the end of 1976, more than 150 Apple computers were sold, giving the company about $95,000 in sales in less than a year. There was something even more important than money, though. Terrell recalled:

> *The Apple I was a great machine for the technically savvy [users] of the time. The Apple I probably had more significance for [Steve and Wozniak] than the customer. [It] gave the two Steves the opportunity to get their act together ... to find out exactly what the market needed without costing the company anything except sweat equity. It was the right product at the right time.* ❖

In 1977, Steve was anxious to unveil his team's latest creation—the Apple II.

CHAPTER SIX

THE BIRTH OF APPLE

EVEN AS THE SALES FOR APPLE I WERE ROLLING in, Woz was already working on an improved version of the computer. Steve couldn't wait to introduce it to the world. Steve and Woz and their small group of friends put every ounce of their talent and energy into making the best Apple computers they could.

Their initial success affirmed Steve's belief that Woz's computer was something special. They planned to sell more of them and make an even better machine. It would be a challenge, requiring greater amounts of their time and risking money they had already earned. Some in the group had doubts. When Steve decided to borrow more money to build more computers, Ron Wayne resigned from the company. He was afraid their business might fail and not be able to pay back the loans.

SHOWTIME IN ATLANTIC CITY

Steve, on the other hand, was confident that the business could grow. His determination and unwavering spirit rubbed off on the others. Steve was inspired by the brilliant improvements Woz had planned for the Apple I. The new machine, called the Apple II, would work with a standard TV so customers wouldn't have to buy a monitor. Woz also engineered the computer to produce color, which was necessary for video games.

Woz also made two more enhancements that would help make the machine widely popular. He engineered a chip to store the BASIC programming language. People wouldn't have to buy BASIC separately or load it every time the machine was turned on. They could start using the computer instantly. Woz also had the good sense to know that computer enthusiasts might want to add more programs to the machine. So he designed the Apple II with eight slots for extra circuit boards.

By August 1976, a prototype of the machine was ready. Steve immediately started proudly showing it off to store owners. One retailer, Stan Veit of Computer Mart, recommended that Steve attend a trade show in Atlantic City, New Jersey, where he could sell more Apple I machines and test the waters for the Apple II.

Steve, Woz, and Dan Kottke arrived in Atlantic City on August 26 for the big event. All the new computer makers were there: MITS, maker of the Altair, had the biggest display. IMSAI's 8080 computers were seen everywhere. Processor Technology's SOL-20, with its built-in keyboard, drew a lot of attention. All of these popular new desktops looked sleek and powerful in their sturdy metal cases.

In contrast, the Apple machines sat on a plain table in a cramped, ordinary booth. The Apple I had a wooden case, which wasn't even sold with the computer. The Apple II prototype, which Steve and Woz were reluctant to show, was rigged up temporarily in a cardboard box. The experience turned out to be a rude awakening. Woz later wrote:

Maybe we weren't part of the business-type groups, but we knew we had a better computer. Actually, we had two better computers, the Apple I and the Apple II. And no one in the world knew about the Apple II yet.

When Steve and Woz left the show they knew that, despite all the work they had done so far, there was a lot left to do. They would need to add a quality keyboard and case and develop the professional-looking displays that the other companies had. They would also need an advertising campaign. All of this would cost money, which they didn't have. The two young wire-

An Apple I is currently housed at the Computer History Museum in Silicon Valley, California.

heads could give up and go back to their regular jobs, or make an even bigger commitment. Woz began to waver, but Steve had the opposite reaction. He had a clear idea of what steps to take next. More importantly, he knew that the Apple II was a better machine than the other computers. They just needed to fine-tune it—and let everyone know how good it was.

A WHOLE NEW LOOK

After leaving the Atlantic City trade show, Steve quickly signed up for another. The next show was in six months, and Steve planned to have the Apple II ready by then. He also wanted a big display booth to show it off. The fact that he couldn't afford the booth—or the necessary improvements to the computer—didn't faze him one bit. He'd find the money somehow.

Steve looked for the best advertising agency he could find to help him make a big splash at the show. His search led him to the Regis McKenna agency, but they turned him down. Steve, however, refused to take no for an answer. He called Regis McKenna's office repeatedly, sometimes several times a day, until McKenna finally agreed to speak with him. McKenna was impressed by his determination and finally agreed to a meeting. Steve's casual clothes—and Woz's lack of interest—nearly killed the deal. Steve refused to leave the office without an agreement to work together, though. Eventually McKenna saw the light. He recalled:

Steve came in and I can remember him sitting in our little conference room and him talking about children using computers and teachers using computers, businesspeople

Steve (left) eventually convinced Regis McKenna (right) to take on Apple Computer as a client. Even though he wondered how or even if he would get paid, McKenna was impressed by Steve's vision.

using computers. He's one of the few people ... I've met in my life who really did envision the future.

McKenna suggested that Apple should have a new logo and recommended artist Rob Janoff. Janoff came up with an image that portrayed quality and simplicity—a rainbow-colored apple with a bite taken out of it. In the meantime, Steve thought about the case. He wanted the Apple II to have a unique look and feel. Instead of choosing a metal case like all the other machines, he decided it should have a beige-colored plastic case and a brown keyboard. He also wanted a quiet computer—one with-

With its beige plastic casing and brown keyboard, the Apple II was unlike any other computer on the market.

out a noisy fan. Most computers require a fan because the power supply generates heat. Steve hired an engineer, Rod Holt, who developed a new power supply device that didn't generate heat. That innovation was patented by Apple. It would be a decade before another Apple computer was made with a fan.

Steve needed money to pay for all these improvements, as well as the cost of advertising. When big investors saw Steve and Woz and the rest of the group working out of the Jobs family garage, they couldn't imagine such a rinky-dink company ever making it big. To attract investors, Steve needed to show them that Apple could be a major player in the computer industry someday. How, Steve wondered, could that be done?

THE APPLE TEAM

Someone at Atari suggested that Steve call Mike Markkula. Markkula was wealthy, but more importantly, he knew about electronics. He instantly recognized that Woz's computer had real potential. Markkula agreed to invest $91,000 of his own money, guarantee a $250,000 loan, and help find other investors. In exchange, he wanted to become a part-owner of Apple.

Woz would have to quit his job at Hewlett-Packard and dedicate himself to Apple. Initially he refused. After much begging by Steve, and more convincing by Markkula, Woz finally agreed.

The men set out to make the Apple II as great as it could be. The company moved from Steve's garage to an office complex in Cupertino, California. They hired Mike Scott as president to handle the finances, and they built up the team to nearly a dozen employees. The group included two recent Homestead High graduates, Randy Wigginton and Chris Espinosa, who were close friends of Woz, along with Bill Fernandez, the person who first introduced the two Steves. Woz and Holt led the effort to fine-tune the machine. Wigginton and Espinosa helped Woz write software programs. Steve focused on the advertising and getting the plastic case made. He also continued to negotiate for the best components at the lowest prices and oversee manufacturing.

Apple's corporate headquarters in Cupertino, California, is located in the heart of Silicon Valley.

By the time the trade show arrived in the spring of 1977, they were ready. They had three Apple II computers for display. Their elaborate booth was located right in the middle of the conference floor. People were amazed that Woz was able to design such a dynamic machine in such a streamlined form. Woz and Steve proudly greeted visitors to the booth and showed off their computer. To make sure the team looked professional, Markkula had insisted that everyone wear a business suit, including Steve. By the end of the show, the Apple team knew it had a hit. With a retail price of $1,298, Apple had introduced the first successful mass market personal computer.

Mike Markkula made a fortune marketing early computer chips. He certainly didn't need a job when Steve came calling, but Markkula couldn't resist the chance to work on groundbreaking products.

The Perfect Partner

Steve and Woz couldn't have found a more perfect business partner than Mike Markkula. An engineer just like them, Markkula had a keen eye for innovative technology. Before joining Apple, he had worked at the two companies—Fairchild Semiconductor and Intel—that introduced the computer chip to the world.

After seeing the Apple computer, Markkula knew that Steve and Woz were onto something revolutionary, and he wanted to be part of it. Markkula not only helped fund the company, but he also served as a mentor to Steve and Woz. He helped them learn how to run a business, and he made important suggestions that improved the Apple computer. For instance, it was Markkula's idea to add a disk drive to the Apple II, a huge factor in the computer's success. Markkula stayed at Apple until 1996.

In the days and weeks after the show, 300 Apple IIs were sold. This doubled the sales total of the first Apple computer in less than one-twelfth of the time. Orders continued to stream in week after week, and by the end of 1977, sales reached 2,500. The company was on firm ground and had several major enhancements in the works. For Steve and Woz, however, the strains of running a business were beginning to show. ❖

The design team behind the Lisa computer worked hard to bring Steve's vision to life.

CHAPTER SEVEN

REACHING NEW HEIGHTS

AT 22 YEARS OLD, MANY YOUNG PEOPLE ARE starting their first jobs or just learning what it means to be an adult. Steve was sitting atop a rapidly growing business in a revolutionary industry. New computer technology was evolving constantly, and there was enormous pressure at Apple to stay a step ahead of the competition. Everyone felt the stress, including Steve. He demanded perfection at every level. This attention to detail often had its benefits, but Steve's demanding temperament could also drive his coworkers crazy.

Steve's friends began to see a new side of him. His instincts had been proven right time after time. Now Steve began to consider his own opinions far more important than anyone else's. He insulted people who disagreed with him. He made fun of good ideas, only to later change his mind or sometimes even claim they were his own. He chewed out people who failed to com-

> **"Back then, [Steve] was uncontrollable. He got ideas in his head, and the [heck] with what anybody else wanted to do."**
>
> – ARTHUR ROCK,
> APPLE BOARD MEMBER

plete work as fast as he thought it should be done. "Back then, he was uncontrollable," recalled Arthur Rock, one of Apple's early board members. "He got ideas in his head, and the [heck] with what anybody else wanted to do."

Steve's personal relationships also suffered. In the summer of 1977, his girlfriend Chris-Ann became pregnant. Steve refused to accept responsibility for the baby girl named Lisa Nicole. It would be many years before Steve finally accepted his daughter into his life.

APPLE RISES TO THE TOP

Amid this turmoil, the team at Apple continued to make amazing enhancements to the Apple II. Woz introduced one innovation that would have a huge impact on personal computers: a disk drive. Disk drives allow people to save their work and use it on another computer. Prior to January 1978, only one other personal computer came with a disk drive.

By mid-1978, there was a two-year waiting list for Apple II computers. The company hired more staff, including salesmen, engineers, programmers, and office workers, to keep pace with demand. In the summer of 1979, to pay for its business expansion, Apple sold shares of its stock worth nearly $7.3 million. As part of that deal, Steve sold shares of his own worth $1 million. At age 24, Steve was a millionaire.

Everyone at Apple was riding the success of the company's first groundbreaking product, but Steve was already looking for the next breakthrough. It wasn't going to be the Apple III, the computer in development at the time. To Steve, the Apple III wasn't the kind of big leap forward he felt the company should be making. To help him make that leap, he hired John Couch and Ken Rothmueller, former engineers at Hewlett-Packard. Together they would begin a project to create a radically different machine. Because every new computer project needed a working title, Steve named this computer Lisa. It was the same name as his 1-year-old daughter, whom Steve still hadn't publicly acknowledged.

Steve (center) often led his design team in a lunchtime huddle to discuss new ideas and ways to improve the products they were working on.

By the late 1970s, Steve—like everyone else at Apple—was riding high on the company's incredible success.

Steve wanted to create the next great computer, and he had no idea of what it might be. For inspiration, he brought a small team to visit Xerox Corporation's Palo Alto Research Center (PARC). Steve had negotiated an agreement with Xerox that allowed the copy machine company to buy shares of Apple in exchange for Apple's right to take at peek at the products Xerox was developing. What Steve saw at Xerox would change personal computers forever.

A GLIMPSE INTO THE FUTURE

Xerox had developed a computer with a screen that resembled a desktop. It displayed menus and windows that worked as folders. Icons helped users identify files and programs. A mouse allowed users to point to and click on the object they wanted to work with. All other computers at the time required users to type a series of commands to do anything. For instance, to copy a file to a disk, a user would have to type *copy c:/filename.txt a:*. Xerox was using the computer in its offices, but had no plans to

More Than Just Copiers

Xerox is a company best known for its office copy machines, which when first introduced in 1959 were a brilliant new technology. Recognizing how important scientific research was to its future, Xerox established a special facility in 1970 dedicated solely to research.

The Palo Alto Research Center (PARC) was founded by physicist George Pake. He chose Palo Alto, California, for the site because he knew it was home to brilliant scientists and engineers. It wasn't long before the researchers at PARC began making technological breakthroughs. In addition to developing the first computer with a mouse and windows-driven screen, which caught the attention of Steve Jobs, PARC researchers came up with many other innovations. These included laser printers, the computer networking technology called Ethernet, and the text editing technology that led to the formation of Adobe Systems. In 2002, PARC became a separate company. It's still owned by Xerox, but it now sells its research capabilities to other companies.

sell it. Steve saw this as a huge opportunity. He wanted to apply Xerox's technology to Lisa's hardware. He knew it would require scrapping all the work that engineers had already done on Lisa and starting over, but he didn't care. Despite arguments from engineers whose work would be lost, Steve insisted on starting over. "Steve has the power of vision that is almost frightening," Trip Hawkins, one of the original members of the Lisa project, later recalled. "When Steve believes in something, the power of that vision can literally sweep aside any objections or problems. They just cease to exist."

> **"Steve has the power of vision that is almost frightening."**
>
> – TRIP HAWKINS, MEMBER OF THE LISA PROJECT TEAM

Steve pushed the engineers to add features or to improve or change the ones the machine already had. He knew it was hard work, but Steve saw how Lisa could change computers forever and tried to instill that vision in his coworkers. "Let's make a dent in the universe," he would say. People inspired by Steve's vision charged ahead. Others complained loudly. Ultimately, Apple's president took the Lisa project away from Steve.

Meanwhile, by the end of 1980, Apple had sold $117 million worth of its software and computers. As investors scrambled to buy shares of Apple stock at around $27 per share, Steve watched his own shares climb to a total value of more than $200 million! The 25-year-old was now among America's super rich.

Steve had fame and fortune, but losing the Lisa project was a huge letdown for him. "It hurt a lot," Steve recalled. "There's

The Lisa was the first computer with a detachable keyboard, mouse, and graphical interface.

no getting around it." He still had the desire to "put a dent in the universe" but nothing to dent it with. Then he was reminded about another project in the works at Apple: the Macintosh.

The Lisa had been designed primarily to use at the office. It was too expensive for the average person. The Macintosh was being engineered as an affordable machine for everyone. It was intended to run on a less expensive and less powerful micro-processor, and it had no graphics capabilities at the time. To a visionary like Steve, this was like taking a deliberate step backward in time. He wondered: Why not make the Macintosh an affordable Lisa? So that's what he set out to do. ❖

In 1983, Steve hired John Sculley (pictured with Steve, left, and Woz, right). He hoped the former Pepsi executive would be able to help Apple outperform IBM.

CHAPTER EIGHT

THE APPLE PIRATES

WHEN STEVE TOOK OVER THE MACINTOSH project, he brought in part of the Apple II team, including Woz, Rod Holt, and Dan Kottke. They joined the group already at work on the Macintosh. The team occupied a suite of offices separate from the rest of the company, and they operated like a band of rebels out to change the world. They even started calling themselves Pirates.

Steve wanted to complete the Macintosh in one year. It was an impossible request, but the staff believed they could do it. This was a classic example of what Apple staffers called Steve's "reality distortion field"—his ability to make people think they could perform the impossible. As Bud Tribble, Apple's manager of software engineering at the time explained, "[Steve] can convince anyone of practically anything. It wears off when he's not around, but it makes it hard to have realistic schedules."

"[Steve] can convince anyone of practically anything."

– BUD TRIBBLE,
SOFTWARE ENGINEER

Steve could inspire workers to do great things, and he rewarded hard work with high praise, expensive parties, special awards, and other benefits. He could also push his staff so hard—sometimes using threats and insults—that workers would burn themselves out or become furious with him. When software engineer Al Hertzfeld joined the team, Tribble spelled out what to expect:

Just because he tells you something is awful or great, it doesn't necessarily mean he'll feel that way tomorrow. He's really funny about ideas. If you tell him a new idea, he'll usually tell you that he thinks it's stupid. But then, if he actually likes it, exactly one week later, he'll come back to you and propose your idea to you, as if he thought of it.

On the other hand, Steve had great admiration for the talent of his team members, and they knew it. Still, Steve pushed people to their limits. His demand for perfection, his habit of changing his mind, and his unrealistic expectations created tension and caused delays. As 1981 came to an end the Mac was nowhere near complete, but things turned around with the new year. By February 1982, the team was gathering steam. That same month, Steve was featured on the cover of *Time* magazine and hailed as one of "America's great risk takers." Less than 12 months later, however, *Time* gave its readers a different view. That article credited Steve for his incredible vision and hard work, but it also aired complaints about him. One Apple staffer said that Steve had a "technical ignorance he's not willing to admit." An anonymous "friend" told the magazine that Steve was growing colder toward people. "Something is happening to Steve that's sad and not pretty," the source said, "something related to money, and power, and loneliness." Woz was quoted as saying "Steve didn't do one circuit, design, or piece of code." The most hurtful comments came from Steve's friend Dan Kottke, who made it public that Steve had a daughter to whom he rarely spoke. To Steve, the comments were jarring. They revealed just how far apart he had drifted from some of his closest friends—and how some of his colleagues resented him.

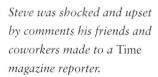

Steve was shocked and upset by comments his friends and coworkers made to a Time *magazine reporter.*

Steve was furious. He called Kottke to complain. Afterward, their friendship was never the same. Steve knew some of the comments were true, including Woz's, but he felt it was wrong to air them in the press. After the incident, he became more private and cautious around the media. He told every employee that if they ever spoke to that journalist again, they would be fired.

A Long Search Ends

While developing the Macintosh, Steve made a startling discovery unrelated to computers. He learned that his biological parents had a second child whom they decided to keep. She was two years younger than Steve, and her name was Mona Simpson. Steve had been looking for his biological parents since he was a teenager. Through a private investigator, Steve finally discovered his natural parents in 1982. He eventually made contact with Mona (pictured) and his biological mother, although the details of how they met remain a secret. Over time, Steve developed a close friendship with his sister, a novelist. He also developed a relationship with his biological mother. Still, he always considered Clara and Paul Jobs his true mom and dad.

BIG BLUE ARRIVES ON THE SCENE

As work on the Mac continued into a second year, Apple's biggest competitor stormed onto the scene. IBM introduced its own personal computer in August 1981. By 1983, IBM had a slightly larger share of the personal computer business than Apple.

In 1983, Steve hired a new chief executive, John Sculley, formerly the president of Pepsi, to help Apple beat the competition. In luring Sculley to Apple, Steve asked "Do you want to spend the rest of your life selling sugared water, or do you want a chance to change the world?"

> **"Do you want to spend the rest of your life selling sugared water, or do you want a chance to change the world?"**
>
> – STEVE JOBS TO JOHN SCULLEY

The comment reflected how Steve saw the computer business—as a way to improve how people lived and worked. Steve sold Sculley on Apple's mission, and the two men made it their mission to sell the Macintosh. They planned one of the most unique product rollouts anyone had ever seen. The most memorable event came during the 1984 Super Bowl, when Apple aired a TV ad based on a theme from the famous novel *1984* by George Orwell. The ad showed a woman racing down the aisle of a room filled with clone-like workers and carrying a sledgehammer. She hurled the sledgehammer at the giant screen image of an all-powerful Big Brother, shattering the image into pieces. The ad took direct aim at IBM, known as Big Blue, and its traditional-looking, traditional-functioning personal computer.

Reimagining the Future

George Orwell's *1984*, published in 1949, was a futuristic look at a society where the actions and opinions of its citizens are monitored and controlled by a dictator known as Big Brother. Conformity and obedience are required.

Apple's advertising agency, Chiat/Day, came up with the slogan "Why 1984 won't be like *1984*." Steve thought it was perfect for a Mac ad. The Mac was meant to give people the ability to express their ideas. It was a weapon to combat conformity. Steve added his own spin, too, comparing Big Brother to Big Blue, the nickname for IBM.

When a group of Apple executives saw a preview of the *1984* ad, they hated it. They wanted to pull it from the airwaves. Chiat/Day said it was too late. The ad, directed by the filmmaker Ridley Scott, became an instant sensation. It won a Clio Award for best TV ad of the year, was named the best ad of the decade by *Advertising Age*, and is still regarded as one of the most brilliant ads ever made.

It wasn't just the ad campaign that was unique. The Macintosh was the first computer made for the general public to use a mouse and menu-driven screen. It included MacWrite, which allowed users for the first time to create documents with different font sizes and styles. MacPaint gave users the ability to draw pictures, which could be cut and pasted into MacWrite documents. It was the first step toward desktop publishing.

When Steve introduced the computer in January 1984, he programmed the Mac to tell a joke. "Never trust a computer you can't lift," the small, lightweight machine said. Steve gave the Mac a personality—cute and funny—and made people think differently about how this machine could transform their lives. Engineer Andy Hertzfeld recalled:

> *The Macintosh never would have happened without him, in anything like the form it did. Other individuals are responsible for the actual creative work, but Steve's vision, passion for excellence, and sheer strength of will, not to mention his awesome powers of persuasion, drove the team to meet or exceed the impossible standards we set for ourselves.*

Steve can be tough on his employees, but he pushes himself just as hard. He is always looking for the next great innovation.

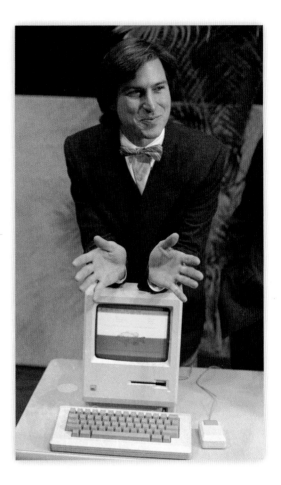

Steve had high hopes for the Macintosh when it was unveiled in 1984.

PUSHED OUT

The Mac wasn't perfect. It had a black-and-white monitor. It wasn't compatible with IBM's PC or even the Lisa. Software made for those computers wouldn't work in a Mac, and very little software was written for the Mac itself. Also, to print the amazing documents and images the Mac produced required a $7,000 printer. The Mac was seen as an expensive toy. The IBM PC was seen as a machine people could use to get work done.

These shortcomings limited the Mac's success. After several months of spectacular sales, the excitement began to fade.

When sales of the Macintosh fell far below expectations, it put the future of Apple at risk. Steve made several attempts to boost sales of the Mac, but they all failed. Many of Apple's executives felt the company had outgrown Steve, as he continued to make bad decisions. Woz, Apple's cofounder, resigned from the company in February 1985 to start a new business. Ironically, less than two weeks later, Woz and Steve were awarded the first ever National Medal of Technology by President Ronald Reagan for introducing the personal computer. Just as they were receiving national recognition for revolutionizing the computer industry, the two founders were going their separate ways.

In May, Apple's board of directors decided that Steve should have a new, smaller role at the company. They named John Sculley to replace him as the chief executive and demoted Steve to the role of an idea man and a spokesperson. Steve realized he had no authority in his new role. Even worse, he had become an outcast at the company he founded. Steve later recalled:

So at 30 I was out. And very publicly out. What had been the focus of my entire adult life was gone, and it was devastating. … I was a very public failure, and I even thought about running away from the valley. But something slowly began to dawn on me—I still loved what I did. The turn of events at Apple had not changed that one bit. … And so I decided to start over. ❖

After being pushed out of Apple, Steve was determined to make his new company—NeXT—a success.

CHAPTER NINE

STARTING OVER

S TEVE WAS PUBLICLY CAST ASIDE BY THE COMPANY he helped create, but he still dreamed of developing the next generation of computers. On September 13, 1985, Steve left Apple. He sold all of his shares in the company except one for more than $100 million. He used $7 million to start a new company called NeXT. The name reflected the unlimited scope of what a computer could become—"the next computing revolution," as Steve would later describe it.

Steve wanted to build a powerful computer that would give a student in a dorm room the same experience as someone in a high-tech lab. He went on a tour of colleges to learn what students would need. Like many of Steve's quests, the journey wouldn't lead where he expected, but it would take him to extraordinary new heights. Steve also had someone to share the adventure. By 1986, he and his daughter were developing a relationship.

UNEXPECTED OPPORTUNITIES

During this period of transition, a unique opportunity was presented to Steve. Back in 1985, when he was still at Apple, Steve went to visit the movie company owned by *Star Wars* creator George Lucas. The company, called Lucasfilm, had a separate division that used computers to create brilliant, high-resolution animated pictures. This group made the special effects for *Star Wars* films. They also did production work for Disney, coloring in drawings by Disney's artists. Steve was instantly impressed by both the computer technology and the talent of the people using it. He wanted to buy the entire computer operation, but at $30 million, the price was too high. Then, in 1986, after Steve had settled in at NeXT, Lucas dropped the price to $10 million. Steve

The NeXT team included former Apple staffers (back row, l to r) Rich Page, Steve Jobs, George Crow, (front, l to r) Dan'l Lewin, Bud Tribble, and Susan Kelly Barnes.

couldn't pass it up. He bought the division, formed a new company, and called it Pixar. His first move was to turn Pixar into a computer company, and start selling the Pixar Image Computer. Along with NeXT, Steve now had two computer businesses to look after. Neither company, however, turned out quite the way Steve imagined they would.

After many delays, Steve finally introduced the NeXT prototype computer in October 1988 to rave reviews. It was unlike any other. The NeXT computer was a perfectly shaped black cube with an enormous 17-inch monitor. It had 16 times more power than a typical computer and used an innovative NeXTStep operating system. The operating system serves as host for all the cool applications a computer can run, and the NeXT computer was loaded with dynamic programs. Unfortunately, not many people could afford the NeXT computer. At a cost of $6,500, it was sold mainly to universities and wealthy businesspeople. Sales never reached expectations, and the company struggled to stay in business. As it turned out, the magic of the NeXT system—the thing that would revolutionize the computer industry—wasn't the cube shape or the 17-inch monitor. It was the NeXTStep operating system. Steve just hadn't realized it yet.

DINNER FOR TWO

In the course of promoting the NeXT computer, Steve made many trips to college campuses. During one visit in 1989, he spoke to students at Stanford University. As Steve spoke, an attractive young woman made her way to the front of the auditorium and sat down. Steve was so mesmerized by the woman that he had trouble remembering what he planned to say. The woman was Laurene Powell, an MBA student at Stanford, and the person who had arranged for Steve to speak there. After the speech, the two met and exchanged business cards. Then Steve had to head off to a business meeting. He never even made it off campus, though, before he changed his mind. Steve later recalled:

> *I was in the parking lot, with the key in the car, and I thought to myself, 'If this is my last night on Earth, would I rather spend it in a business meeting or with this woman?' I ran across the parking lot, [and] asked her if she'd have dinner with me.*

Laurene agreed and the two began seeing a lot of each other. On March 18, 1991, they were married. Presiding over the wedding was a Buddhist monk, Kobin Chino, who had been Steve's mentor for years. Less than a year later, the couple moved to a home in Palo Alto and had their first child, Reed Paul Jobs. Their son was named after Reed College and Steve's father, Paul. Steve and Laurene would have two more children together, Erin Sienna, born in 1995, and Eve, born in 1998.

While Steve was finding happiness in his personal life, business matters were reaching a crisis stage. He still couldn't figure out what to do with Pixar. At first, he thought he could sell Pixar's computer system. As a way to show off the machine, Pixar's animation team, led by John Lasseter, used it to developed short films. The first, called *Luxo Jr.*, about a mischievous desk lamp, was produced in 1986. The film earned Lasseter an Academy Award nomination. Unfortunately, it didn't sell many

Laurene had much in common with Steve. She was very smart, ate a vegetarian diet, and kept fit. She also had an interest in Zen Buddhism.

computers. The Pixar machine was simply too expensive and too complex for even big businesses. Pixar earned some money by selling its digital picture-making and storage capabilities to companies like Disney. The money generated wasn't enough to prevent Pixar from falling deeper in debt, though.

To keep the company from going bankrupt, Steve had it stop making computers altogether. Then he sold off nearly all of the company's assets. He even considered getting rid of the animation team. In 1989, Lasseter won an Oscar for a short film called *Tin Toy*. The award gave Steve hope that the animation department was worth holding onto—but it still wasn't paying the bills.

The huge success of Toy Story *gave new life to Pixar.*

MAKING MOVIES

Steve needed to get out of the financial hole, and Pixar's team dreamed of making full-length movies. Steve found a solution to both problems by making a deal with the Walt Disney company. In May 1991, he signed a contract for Pixar to do three animated movies for $5 million each. Disney would get more than 85 percent of the profit from each film. It was a horrible deal for Pixar, but the agreement provided the cash needed to stay in business and a project to demonstrate the company's moviemaking talents. Pixar's first project for Disney would be a movie called *Toy Story.*

While Pixar struggled to find its footing, Steve's dream of making NeXT into a great computer company was fading into a nightmare. NeXT was losing money and showing no signs of ever making any. In 1993, Steve was forced to close the high-tech NeXT manufacturing plant he had built. He had to sell off everything in it, right down to the paper shredders and trash cans. As he did with Pixar, Steve held onto the one thing that was bringing in cash—the NeXTStep operating system—but it was a poor consolation prize. For Steve, the demise of NeXT was another public failure, making it appear as if his success at Apple was just an accident.

Steve was dealt another blow in 1993 when Disney decided to stop production on *Toy Story*. Lasseter's team was forced to scramble to figure out how to make the lead character, a toy cowboy named Woody, more likeable. Lasseter spent months thinking about the problem before deciding to add a new beginning to the movie. The new footage showed Woody as a little boy's best friend and the leader of his fellow toys. Fortunately, Disney liked the changes, and work continued. Early the next year, after seeing a preview of the film, Steve knew that *Toy Story* would be a winner. He was right. *Toy Story* was a huge hit. The movie took four long years to make, but Jobs never gave up on the project or his team. Pixar's cofounder Edwin Catmull said:

You need a lot more than vision—you need a stubbornness, tenacity, belief, and patience to stay the course. In Steve's case, he pushes right to the edge, to try to make the next big step forward. It's built into him.

Master Negotiator

With *Toy Story* at the peak of its popularity, Steve went to Disney and renegotiated Pixar's contract. He threatened to make movies for Disney's competitors if the company didn't agree to a more equal share of movie profits. Afraid of losing Pixar, Disney executives agreed to share profits equally. They also agreed to give John Lasseter full creative control of the movies he made. Pixar, once on the verge of bankruptcy, was now on its way to making one blockbuster hit after another, including *A Bug's Life, Toy Story 2, Monsters, Inc., Finding Nemo, The Incredibles,* and *Cars.* Eventually, Pixar and Disney would merge into one company, with Steve becoming its largest shareholder.

HOMECOMING

The success of Pixar took some of the sting out of NeXT's collapse, and Steve still had the NeXTStep operating system. In 1993, he turned NeXT into NeXT Software, Inc., and focused the business on creating operating systems for other companies. One company in particular expressed a keen interest in NeXT Software. That company was Apple Computer.

After Steve left Apple in 1985, the company lost its reputation for developing groundbreaking products. In 1990, Microsoft introduced Windows 3.0 for the PC, attempting to copy the look and feel of the Mac. That marked the beginning of big trouble for Apple. Without a visionary like Steve, Apple found itself stuck in time with no new computer to excite its customers.

After all the bad feelings surrounding Steve's departure from Apple, it seemed unlikely that he would be willing to return. In 1985, however, amid the turmoil of being pushed aside as Apple's leader, Steve told a reporter:

I'll always stay connected with Apple. I hope that throughout my life I'll sort of have the thread of my life and the thread of Apple weave in and out of each other like a tapestry. There may be a few years when I'm not there, but I'll always come back.

Steve didn't find success with the NeXT computer, but the software would lead him back to Apple.

In December 1996, Gil Amelio, Apple's chief executive, made a deal with Steve to buy NeXT Software for $400 million and bring Steve in as an adviser. "I'm not just buying the software," Amelio said at the time. "I'm buying Steve." It didn't take long, however, for Apple's board members to realize that Steve represented Apple's future. After about six months, he replaced Amelio as head of the company.

> **"I'm not just buying the [NeXT] software. I'm buying Steve."**
>
> – GIL AMELIO,
> FORMER APPLE CEO

Steve wasted little time in making big changes. To restore Apple's image as a fun, dynamic company, he introduced a $100 million ad campaign around the slogan "Think Different." Steve also developed an important new relationship with one of his former rivals, Microsoft, to ensure that company would continue creating software for the Mac. He then began weeding out all the products that he thought were a waste of money, focusing on only the dozen or so he thought could be truly great.

One of the products Steve kept was the iMac. The machine was designed to give people easy, instant access to the Web, including e-mail. The Internet gave millions of people a reason to buy a computer, and Steve wanted to have the perfect machine to get them up and running. For many, the iMac was it.

In April 1998, Steve introduced the iMac. Apple received more than 150,000 orders before it even went on sale. The company sold 278,000 iMacs in less than two months, and two million in the first year. Clearly, Apple was back. So was Steve. By 2000, Steve had accepted the official role of chief executive.

Bill Gates: Competitor and Partner

While Steve and Woz were developing the Apple I, Bill Gates was doing his part to revolutionize the computer industry, too. In 1975, Gates dropped out of college to start Microsoft. He and cofounder Paul Allen had created the popular programming language Altair BASIC. Their success led IBM to ask Microsoft to develop an operating system for its PC. Soon, Microsoft's operating system, MS-DOS, became a standard for all other personal computers—except Apple's.

In 1981, Microsoft developed Windows, an operating system that mimicked the look and feel of a Mac. In 1994, Apple unsuccessfully sued Microsoft for copying the look of the Mac. By 1997, Steve and Gates were working cooperatively. Microsoft partnered with Apple to develop software for

Jobs and Gates started out as competitors. By 1997, however, they were working together on software for Apple computers.

the new Macs, which helped Apple's resurgence. "I sort of look at us as the two luckiest guys on the planet," Steve has said, "We found what we loved to do and we were at the right place at the right time."

THE DIGITAL HUB

The iMac was just the beginning of a new wave of great gadgets Apple would produce. In the late 1990s, technology was rapidly changing. The Internet, DVDs, digital cameras, and cell phones were bursting onto the scene, transforming sound and images into digital components. Steve saw how these innovations were changing the way people lived and worked—creating a "digital lifestyle." Steve and Apple realized that the computer was central to this lifestyle. Apple called it the "digital hub."

Apple began designing applications like iMovie, iTunes, and iPhoto for Mac users to share, organize, and edit their digital world. Steve also realized that people wanted to take their digital world with them wherever they went—especially their favorite music. So Apple set its sights on creating a portable music player. In October 2001, Steve introduced the iPod. It was an instant sensation, capable of holding 1,000 songs in a sleek white box the size of a deck of cards. When Apple made the iPod compatible with Windows systems, sales began to soar.

TRAGEDY AND TRIUMPH

By 2003, Steve Jobs was at the top of the computer world. He and his wife Laurene were living happily with their children, and Steve had a relationship with his oldest daughter, Lisa. Then, in an instant, it all seemed to go up in smoke. In October 2003, Steve was diagnosed with pancreatic cancer. "The doctors told me ... that I should expect to live no longer than three to six months," he recalled. "My doctor told me to go home and get my affairs in order, which is doctor's code for prepare to die."

A Music Revolution

It would seem natural that record companies would want to sell music over the Internet, but for many years, they didn't. They worried people would steal their music—and they were right. For years, people used file-sharing programs to illegally download music. Steve's solution was the iTunes Music Store. People could pay 99 cents to download a song, but the song could only be played in iTunes, on an iPod, or copied onto a CD. By inserting a special program called FairPlay in each music file, Apple was able to limit the number of computers that songs could be downloaded to and the number of times it could be copied onto a CD. This solved the file-sharing problem.

It took Apple a year and a half to reach a deal with the record companies and get the store up and running. In April 2003, the iTunes Music Store was launched with 200,000 songs in its library. Within a week, more than a million songs were sold. Today, iTunes also sells movies, TV shows, music videos, and more.

Over the years, Apple has teamed with many musicians, including U2's Bono, to promote the iPod and iTunes.

Shortly after detecting the tumor, doctors performed a biopsy so they could examine the cells of the tumor more closely. They were amazed—and relieved—by what they found. It turned out Steve had a very rare form of pancreatic cancer that is curable with surgery. In July 2004, Steve had surgery to remove the cancer and recovered fully.

Steve's experience with cancer left a lasting impression. During a commencement speech at Stanford University in 2005, Steve shared those impressions and offered this advice:

Your time is limited, so don't waste it by living someone else's life. Don't be trapped by dogma—which is living with the results of other people's thinking. Don't let the noise of others' opinions drown out your own inner voice. And most important, have the courage to follow your heart and intuition.

WHAT WILL THE FUTURE HOLD?

Steve continues to live by those words. Along with the release of the iPhone in 2007 came news of Apple TV, a device that transfers music, movies, and TV shows from the computer to a television set. Apple also has already filed patents for solar cell technology that can be used with portable electronic devices like its ultra thin laptop, the MacBook Air, and its iPod and iPhone. Will solar-powered laptops be the next big thing? Or will something completely different take the computer world by storm? It's impossible to know, but one can be sure that Steve Jobs is thinking about it.

Steve is always looking toward the future for the next big technological breakthrough.

"There's an old Wayne Gretzky quote that I love," Steve said. "'I skate to where the puck is going to be, not where it has been.' And we've always tried to do that at Apple, since the very beginning. And we always will." ❖

TIME LINE

1955 Steve is born on February 24 in San Francisco, California, and is adopted by Paul and Clara Jobs.

1965 Steve begins visiting the workshop of neighbor and electronics engineer Larry Lange. At the suggestion of Mr. Lange, Steve joins the Hewlett-Packard Explorers Club. There he gets an inside look at H-P's latest inventions.

1967 Steve sees his first personal computer at a meeting of the H-P Explorers Club. The Jobs family moves to Los Altos, California, where Steve becomes friends with Bill Fernandez. Bill introduces Steve to his friend Steve "Woz" Wozniak.

1968 Steve enrolls at Homestead High School and joins the electronics club. Woz and Bill build a computer from scratch.

1971 Steve and Woz start their first business together—making illegal boxes that provide free long-distance phone calls.

1972 Steve enrolls in Reed College in Portland, Oregon, but drops out after six months. He decides to audit classes for no credit.

1973 Steve takes his first trip to the All-One Farm, where he helps tend an apple orchard.

1974 A lack of money forces Steve to return to his parent's house. He takes a job at Atari, engineering video games. That summer, he and his friend Dan Kottke take a month-long journey to India.

1975 *Popular Electronics* magazine features a story on a do-it-yourself computer called the Altair. Steve and Woz work together to sell Woz's homemade computers.

1976 Steve, Woz, and Ron Wayne form Apple Computer in April. Woz designs the company's first computer, Apple I; by the end of the year they've sold more than 150 machines. Steve and Woz attend their first trade show in Atlantic City. Steve then hires the Regis McKenna advertising agency to revamp the company's image. Mike Markkula becomes a major investor—and partner—in Apple.

1977 Apple introduces the first successful mass market personal computer (Apple II) at a San Francisco trade show.

1979 Apple stock goes on sale to pay for the company's expansion. Steve is a millionaire at age 24. He begins work on the Lisa project.

1980 Steve is taken off the Lisa project and moves to the Macintosh team.

1984 Steve introduces the Macintosh in January.

1985 Woz resigns from Apple in February; Steve and Woz receive the National Medal of Technology. In May, Steve is replaced as chief executive; he formally leaves Apple on September 13.

1986 Steve starts a new computer company, NeXT, and buys Pixar.

1993 Steve is forced to shut down NeXT's computer manufacturing plant; he focuses on selling the NeXT software system.

1996 Steve returns to Apple in December and quickly turns the ailing company around.

1998 Steve introduces the iMac, a computer designed for easy Internet access, in April.

2001 Steve introduces the iPod, a portable music device, in October.

2003 Steve is diagnosed with pancreatic cancer but recovers.

2007 Steve introduces the iPhone at the Macworld Conference & Expo.

2008 Steve introduces the MacBook Air—the world's thinnest laptop—at Macworld.

A CONVERSATION WITH
Steve Wozniak

 *Steve Wozniak started Apple Computer with his good friend Steve Jobs in 1976. Together, they revolutionized the computer industry. Here, Woz talks about what it was like to be at the very center of the technological revolution that changed the world.*

Q: What made you like computers so much?

A: Nobody, not even a parent, showed me anything about computers. I stumbled onto [them] by accident, and [they were] my secret love, even though I didn't think I'd ever work on them myself. ... In high school I [was given] a great privilege to program a computer at a company. We didn't have them in schools back then. ... It became a game of mine to design computers on paper. ... I did it silently and secretly and made up a game to design them better and better, with fewer and fewer parts. I eventually came up with abilities that I thought few others in the world had.

Q: What were your impressions of Steve when you first met? What made you become friends?

A: We became instant friends. We both knew digital chips, which was rare in those days. We both liked playing pranks. We both opposed and questioned authority. We liked the deep meaning of Bob Dylan songs and other songs with messages about life. Although I was five years older than Steve Jobs ...

we were both at that point in life when some get serious about what is right and wrong and what are the guides to living your life.

Q: Why did you decide to go into business together? What made you think it would work?

A: I had designed my own computer that could really run programs that you type in. It was the achievement of my lifetime dream. I gave my designs away for free at a club of people, some of whom had the skills to assemble it. Steve ... suggested that we sell a PC board for $40 to help them wire these computers faster and easier. We didn't know that we'd sell enough PC boards to make money, maybe 50 PC boards, but it didn't matter. We two best friends would have our own company for once in our lives.

I would not sell something of my design without offering it to my company, Hewlett-Packard, first. They turned me down ... so Steve and I started Apple.

Q: You and Steve became successful very fast. What was that like?

A: The Apple II was my first real computer, designed from the ground up. It was a revolutionary invention. Along with financing came a requirement for me to leave [my job at Hewlett-Packard]. I only did so under the terms that I would be nothing other than an engineer for life. I would not run the company. Steve Jobs would learn to run every department of a company. So we worked on different things from then on. I was the engineer, and he was the businessman.

Q: How did success affect your relationship with Steve?

A: The wealth hits you slowly. I had such a strong ethical background (from my father) that I didn't want money. I wanted to be in the middle.

[My relationship with Steve] changed. We did different things. Steve was more devoted to leading the world in new directions. I was great at my engineering, but once Apple had dozens of engineers I wasn't single-handedly critical to the company.

Steve and I have always maintained our friendship but it's not close. We have our own lives. We respect each other greatly.

Q: Some found it hard to work with Steve. What were the best—and worst—things about working with him?

A: [I] always found him very thoughtful about strategies and product directions. He was a bit impatient, but our angel investor, Mike Markkula, who ran marketing, was a good mentor. I never had the sort of difficulties others described with Steve. He has been respectful to me almost on every occasion.

Q: What's your relationship with Steve today?

A: Friends with great memories.

Q: What advice do you have for young people interested in electronics or inventing things?

A: Find kits to start with. Making your own things makes you a superman when you are young.

GLOSSARY

audit: to attend a class under no obligation to do assigned classwork, and for no credit

biopsy: to remove a body tissue sample for medical diagnosis; or the sample itself

calligraphy: decorative handwriting; the art of writing

circuit board: a flat piece of material on which integrated circuits and other electrical components are printed or installed

demoted: relegated to a lower position

dogma: a belief, or set of beliefs, put forth as true

font: a set of letters or characters of the same size and style

frequency counter: an electrical device that measures the number or cycles or waves per a unit of time

guru: a Hindu teacher, instructor, or spiritual leader

hacker: a person who uses a computer to gain unauthorized access to computer systems

hologram: a three-dimensional image of an object made using lasers and photographic plates

innovative: provoking change

icon: an image or a symbol, such as a symbol on a computer monitor that represents a command

interface: an interconnection between systems, equipment, concepts, or human beings

intuition: a gut feeling

logo: a name or an image that is easily recognized as representing a company or organization

machinist: a person who operates a machine or uses machine tools

mentor: a wise and helpful counselor or teacher

microprocessor: a computer's central processing unit (CPU), which interprets and runs a computer's programs, fabricated on a single integrated circuit

oscillator: a device through which energy, such as an electric current, moves in regulated cycles or frequencies

prototype: an original model, typically in its early stages of development

revamped: reconstructed, revised, renovated

rudiments: fundamental elements, principles, or skills

sans serif: a kind of letter, character, or typeface without a serif, which is a tiny line added at the end of the main stroke of a character

schematic: a diagram, or drawing of a plan, typically used to outline mechanical or electrical systems

silicon chip: an integrated circuit made on a silicon substrate, or base; also known as a microchip, a chip, or an integrated circuit

solder: join two pieces of metal together using molten metal or metallic alloy

tedious: tiresome and dull; boring

FOR MORE INFORMATION

BOOKS AND OTHER RESOURCES

Brackett, Virginia. *Steve Jobs: Computer Genius of Apple*. Berkeley Heights, New Jersey: Enslow Publishers, March 2003.

Hertzfeld, Andy. *Revolution in the Valley: The Insanely Great Story of How the Mac Was Made*. Sebastopol, California: O'Reilly Media, Inc., December 2004.

Lemkie, Donald B. *Steve Jobs, Steve Wozniak, and the Personal Computer*. Mankato, Minnesota: Capstone Press, January 2007.

Wilson, Suzan. *Steve Jobs: Wizard of Apple Computer*. Berkeley Heights, New Jersey: Enslow Publishers, September 2001.

Wozniak, Steve, with Gina Smith. *iWoz*. New York: W. W. Norton and Company, 2006.

WEB SITES

Apple Events
www.apple.com/quicktime/guide/appleevents/
Watch Apple CEO Steve Jobs personally introduce some of the company's newest products.

The Apple Museum
www.theapplemuseum.com
This site is dedicated to the history of Apple computers and the people who introduced them to the world. Includes biographies of the Apple staff, as well as images of Apple computers dating back to the very first models.

SELECT BIBLIOGRAPHY AND SOURCE NOTES

Hertzfeld, Andy. *Revolution in the Valley: The Insanely Great Story of How the Mac Was Made.* Sebastopol, Calif.: O'Reilly Media, December 2004.

Smithsonian Institution Oral and Video Histories, *Interview with Steve Jobs,* April 20, 1995.

Wozniak, Steve, with Gina Smith. *iWoz.* N.Y.: W. W. Norton and Company, 2006.

Young, Jeffrey S. *Steve Jobs: The Journey Is the Reward.* Glenview, Ill.: Foresman and Company, 1988.

PAGE 2

Jobs, Steve. Commencement speech at Stanford University, June 12, 2005, transcript published by *Stanford Report,* June 14, 2005, accessed at http://news-service. stanford.edu/news/2005/june15/ jobs-061505.html

CHAPTER ONE

Page 8, line 3: Apple.com, Macworld San Francisco 2007 keynote address, accessed at http://www. apple.com/quicktime/qtv/mwsf07
Page 8, line 20: Ibid.
Page 11, line 3: "Dial and Shuffle," CNN, January 10, 2007, accessed at http://www.dailymotion.com/ relevance/search/STEVEJOBS_ IPHONE_2007_CNN/video/ xyybu_stevejobsiphone2007cnn_ events

CHAPTER TWO

Page 16, line 14: Smithsonian Institution Oral and Video Histories, *Interview with Steve Jobs,* April 20, 1995
Page 17, line 7: Ibid.
Page 17, line 17: Ibid.
Page 17, line 26: Young, Jeffrey S. *Steve Jobs: The Journey Is the Reward.* Glenview, Ill.: Foresman and Company, 1988, p. 24
Page 18, line 4: Ibid.
Page 21, line 26: Smithsonian Institution Oral and Video Histories, *Interview with Steve Jobs,* April 20, 1995
Page 23, sidebar: Wozniak, Steve, with Gina Smith. *iWoz.* N.Y.: W. W. Norton and Company, 2006, pp. 88–89

CHAPTER THREE

Page 25, line 8: Smithsonian Institution Oral and Video Histories, *Interview with Steve Jobs,* April 20, 1995
Page 27, line 8: Young. *Steve Jobs: The Journey Is the Reward,* p. 29
Page 27, line 20: Ibid.
Page 29, line 15: Wozniak. *iWoz,* p. 89
Page 29, line 21: Young. *Steve Jobs: The Journey Is the Reward,* p. 37
Page 33, line 23: Lohr, Steve. "Creating Jobs," *The New York Times,* January 12, 1997

CHAPTER FOUR

Page 35, line 13: Young. *Steve Jobs: The Journey Is the Reward,* p. 52
Page 36, line 5: Jobs. Commencement speech at Stanford University
Page 36, line 19: Ibid.
Page 37, line 8: Ibid.
Page 37, sidebar: Schwartz, Todd. "The Dance of the Pen," *Reed Magazine,* August 2003
Page 38, line 7: Jobs. Commencement speech at Stanford University
Page 39, line 9: Randall, Stephen, and the editors of *Playboy* magazine,

ed. "1985 interview by David Sheff," *The Playboy Interviews: Movers and Shakers.* Chicago, Ill.: Playboy Enterprises International, p. 98

Page 40, line 13: Young. *Steve Jobs: The Journey Is the Reward*, p. 60

Page 42, line 19: Ibid., p. 66

CHAPTER FIVE

Page 45, line 4: Young. *Steve Jobs: The Journey Is the Reward*, p. 71

Page 49, line 15: Wozniak. *iWoz*, p. 172

Page 51, line 4: Ibid.

Page 52, line 5: Young. *Steve Jobs: The Journey Is the Reward*, p. 94

Page 53, line 19: McCracken, Harry. *PC World* Techblog, August 23, 2007

CHAPTER SIX

Page 57, line 7: Wozniak. *iWoz*, p. 189

Page 58, line 24: Interview with Regis McKenna, Stanford University library, August 22, 1995, http://www-sul.stanford.edu/depts/hasrg/histsci/silicongenesis/regis-ntb.html

CHAPTER SEVEN

Page 66, line 2: Elkind, Peter. "The Trouble with Steve Jobs," *Fortune Magazine*, March 5, 2008

Page 70, line 6: Young. *Steve Jobs: The Journey Is the Reward*, p. 176

Page 70, line 18: Ibid., p. 187

Page 70, line 28: Ibid., p. 191

CHAPTER EIGHT

Page 73, line 13: Hertzfeld, Andy. "Reality Distortion Field," Folklore.org

Page 74, line 11: Ibid.

Page 75, line 2: Cocks, Jay. "The Updated Book of Jobs," *Time*, January 3, 1983

Page 75, line 4: Ibid.

Page 75, line 6: Ibid.

Page 77, line 11: "Triumph of the Nerds," PBS

Page 79, line 4: Hertzfeld, Andy. *Revolution in the Valley: The Insanely Great Story of How the Mac Was Made.* Sebastopol, Calif.: O'Reilly Media, December 2004, p. 222

Page 79, line 9: Hertzfeld, Andy. "The Father of the Macintosh," Folklore.org

Page 81, line 20: Jobs. Commencement speech at Stanford University, June 12, 2005

CHAPTER NINE

Page 83, line 7: Patton, Phil. "Steve Jobs: Out for Revenge," *The New York Times*, August 6, 1989

Page 86, line 7: Lohr. "Creating Jobs"

Page 89, line 24: Ibid.

Page 91, line 7: Randall, Stephen, et. al. (ed.) "1985 interview by David Sheff," *The Playboy Interviews: Movers and Shakers*, p. 109

Page 92, line 3: Lohr. "Creating Jobs"

Page 93, sidebar: Interview with Walt Mossberg and Kara Swisher, *Wall Street Journal*, June 1, 2007, accessed at http://online.wsj.com/article/SB118066046287520886.html?mod=googlenews_wsj

Page 94, line 24: Jobs. Commencement speech at Stanford University, June 12, 2005

Page 96, 10: Ibid.

Page 97, line 1: Apple.com, Macworld San Francisco 2007 keynote address

INDEX

ABOUT THE AUTHOR

Tony Imbimbo is a writer and editor who lives in Darien, Connecticut with his wife, Kristen, and daughters Elsa and Sofia. He has written about topics ranging from sports and music to history and science. Coauthor of the book *Magnets and Electromagnetism*, his work has also appeared in magazines such as *Sports Illustrated* and *Seventeen*. He has a degree in journalism from Syracuse University and an MBA from the University of Connecticut. He wrote much of this book using a Mac, occasionally while listening to iTunes.

PICTURE CREDITS